DISCOVERING CLAMS

Lorijo Metz

PowerKiDS press.

New York

For Papa Metz, may you live as long and be as happy as a clam!

Published in 2012 by The Rosen Publishing Group, Inc.
29 East 21st Street, New York, NY 10010

First Edition

Editor: Amelie von Zumbusch
Book Design: Kate Laczynski

Photo Credits: Cover, p. 8 © Marevision/age fotostock; p. 4 Vincenzo Lombardo/Getty Images; pp. 5, 12 Comstock Images/Comstock/Thinkstock; p. 6 Jupiterimages/Photos.com/Thinkstock; pp. 7 (top), 11, 16, 17 (top), 19, 22 Shutterstock.com; p. 7 (bottom) Darlyne A. Murawski/Getty Images; p. 9 Daniel Gotshall/Getty Images; p. 10 David Wrobel/Getty Images; pp. 13, 17 (bottom) iStockphoto/Thinkstock; p. 14 Christopher Seufert Photography/Getty Images; p. 15 Richard J. Murphy/Getty Images; p. 18 © www.iStockphoto.com/ Harry Thomas; p. 20 MPI/Getty Images; p. 21 Kathrin Ziegler/Getty Images.

Library of Congress Cataloging-in-Publication Data

Metz, Lorijo.
 Discovering clams / by Lorijo Metz. — 1st ed.
    p. cm. — (Along the shore)
 Includes index.
 ISBN 978-1-4488-4994-9 (library binding)
 1. Clams—Juvenile literature. I. Title.
 QL430.6.M48 2012
 594'.4—dc22
                                   2011000158

Manufactured in the United States of America

CPSIA Compliance Information: Batch #WS11PK: For Further Information contact Rosen Publishing, New York, New York at 1-800-237-9932

CONTENTS

HARD SHELLS AND SOFT BODIES

Imagine living for over 400 years! Some clams live that long. In fact, scientists think that a **species**, or type, of clam known as the ocean quahog is the longest-living animal on Earth!

Clams are **mollusks**. The word "mollusk" comes from *mollis*, which is the Latin word for "soft." Mollusks have soft bodies. Most have shells, too.

You can see the soft body of the clam with the open shell here. The other clams' bodies are hidden inside their hard shells.

These divers are looking at a giant clam. These clams' shells have wavy edges. Every giant clam's coloring is a little bit different.

Clams are **bivalve** mollusks. Bivalve mollusks have two hard shells. Other bivalve mollusks include oysters, scallops, and mussels.

Most clams are between .5 inch and 4 inches (1–10 cm) wide. One species, called the giant clam, often grows to be up to 4 feet (1 m) long. It can weigh more than 500 pounds (227 kg).

WHERE DO CLAMS LIVE?

Most clams live on the sandy, muddy bottom of the ocean floor. Northern quahogs live along the Atlantic coast of North America. People use them to make a rich soup called clam chowder.

Other clams, such as Pacific gaper clams, live in **mudflats** along the Pacific coast. During high

Many clams live in mudflats along the coast. These mudflats are along the Pacific Ocean in Marin County, California.

The Great Barrier Reef is home to this giant clam. This huge coral reef system is in the waters off of northeastern Australia.

tide, seawater covers these muddy strips of land. It leaves behind a rich layer of food for clams and other animals.

Giant clams live on **coral reefs** in the South Pacific Ocean and Indian Ocean. Coral reefs build up when tiny animals called corals grow on top of the remains of older corals.

Amethyst gem clams live along North America's Atlantic coast. They are very small. The clams are mixed with grains of sand in this close-up picture.

WHAT DO CLAMS LOOK LIKE?

A thin, skinlike covering called the **mantle** covers a clam's soft body. The mantle produces the chalklike matter that makes up a clam's shells. The two hard shells join at the back. They open and close with the aid of two strong muscles.

This is a Venus clam. You can see the clam's mantle along the top and bottom of the shell. Its siphons are to the left and its foot to the right.

You can see the siphons of some Pacific gaper clams here. The rest of the clams' bodies are buried in the mud, though.

Clams do not have a head or arms. Inside their shells, they have a heart, a stomach, and a muscle called a foot. The foot sticks out between a clam's shells. It helps the clam move and dig. Water and food enter and leave the clam through two tubelike parts of the mantle, called **siphons**.

EATING TO BREATHE AND BREATHING TO EAT

Clams are filter feeders. Filter feeders keep water clean by eating tiny plants and animals called **plankton**.

Like fish, clams use **gills** to breathe. Like all animals, they breathe **oxygen**. Clams eat and breathe at the same time. To do this, they reach

These siphons belong to a piddock clam. The two siphons have different jobs. While one takes in water, the other lets it out.

Like all animals that breathe with gills, clams need to stay wet to stay alive. Their gills can take in oxygen only from water.

into the water with their tubelike siphons. First, they draw in water full of plankton through one siphon. As the water flows in, the gills take oxygen from it. At the same time, tiny hairlike parts on the gills trap plankton and pass it along for the clams to eat. Finally, the second siphon pumps the water back into the ocean.

HOW DO CLAMS GROW?

Clams produce eggs in late spring, when the water begins to warm. Female clams pump thousands, or even millions, of eggs into the water through their siphons. Only a few eggs will go on to become **larvae**, or baby clams. Of those, only a few will become adults.

Some young clams attach themselves to rocks or sand with

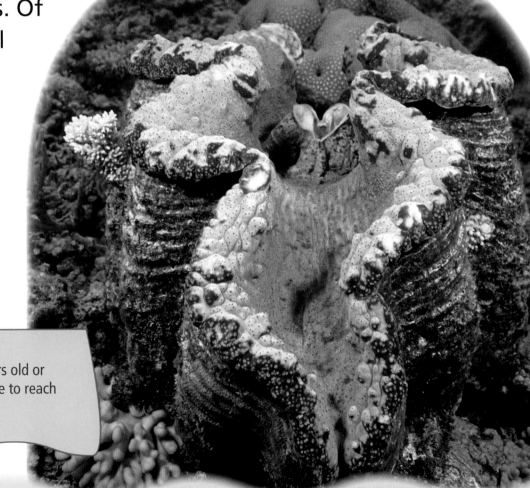

Giant clams can live to be 100 years old or older. This gives them plenty of time to reach their huge size!

The more rings a clam's shell has, the older the clam is. The rings near the shell's edge are the newest. The rings near the umbo are the oldest.

their **byssus**. This is a threadlike fiber they produce. Others use their feet to dig into the seafloor.

The oldest part of a clam's shell is the umbo. This is the bump on the back of its shell. One way to tell a clam's age is by counting the number of growth rings on its outer shell.

MANY KINDS OF CLAMS

Some clams have very hard shells. Others have thin shells that break easily. Clams with thin shells often do not close fully because their siphons stick out of the side. Two clams with thin shells are steamer clams and Pacific razor clams. Steamer clams live in mudflats along the Atlantic coast. Pacific razor clams are found on sandy beaches from California to Alaska.

This northern quahog is from Cape Cod, Massachusetts. The word "quahog" likely comes from the animal's Narragansett Indian name, *poquauhock*.

This Pacific razor clam was dug up on a beach in Ninilchik, Alaska. These clams are often caught to be sold. People also catch the clams to eat themselves.

CLAM FACT

Pacific gaper clams, or horse clams, have hard shells. They live in mudflats along Oregon's coast. Their long siphons let them live deep under the sand.

Northern quahogs have hard shells. In fact, they are also called hard-shell clams. These clams have names based on their size, too. Small ones are called littlenecks, larger ones are cherrystones, and chowder clams are ones that are at least 3 inches (8 cm) wide.

15

CLAMS AND PREDATORS

Clams guard themselves from predators by closing their hard shells around their soft bodies. Giant clams have special skin that can sense movement. They also have simple eyes, which sense shadows, lining the outer edge of their mantle. By sensing movement and shadows, they have time to close their large shells before predators attack.

This sea otter is eating the soft body of a clam it caught. Clams are one of the foods that sea otters eat most often.

Crabs can open clamshells with their powerful claws. Then they can eat the soft meat inside.

Even with their hard shells, animals such as starfish, seagulls, and even snails eat clams. Otters have an interesting way of eating clams. While floating on its back, an otter will place a rock on its belly. Then it will smash the clam against the rock to open it.

Clams are an important food for walruses. Walruses suck clams from their shells. They may eat as many as 6,000 clams at a time!

CLAM DIGGING AND FARMING

In the state of Washington, digging for clams is a well-liked family outing. On nice days, thousands of people line beaches to dig up Pacific razor clams. All you need is a shovel, a bucket, boots to keep your feet dry, and a state clam license. Sometimes clams can be **overharvested**. This happens when people collect

This woman is gathering clams in Coos Bay, Oregon. Pacific gaper clams, Pacific littleneck clams, Pacific razor clams, and butter clams all live in Coos Bay.

People all around the world dig for clams. These people are digging up clams along the shore in Awase, on the Japanese island of Okinawa.

too many clams, making it hard for the species to grow back.

Some people raise their own clams. In places such as Cedar Key, Florida, clam farming is a big business. Since clams clean the water as they feed, clam farming is good for the environment. Raising clams also helps cut down on overharvesting.

PEOPLE AND CLAMS

For thousands of years, Native Americans used shells, including northern quahog clamshells, to make beads called wampum. Strung together or made into belts, wampum served many important purposes. People even used it as money.

People eat clams in many different ways. As far back as the 1700s, people made soups that are

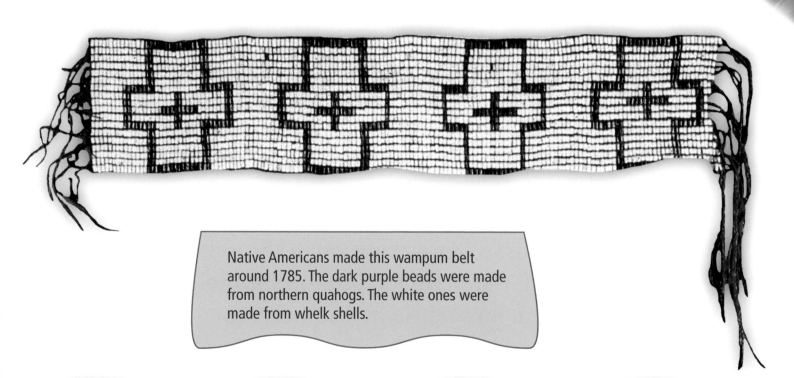

Native Americans made this wampum belt around 1785. The dark purple beads were made from northern quahogs. The white ones were made from whelk shells.

These people are eating clams at a restaurant along the beach. Clams are often served at restaurants along the coast.

CLAM FACT

Japanese people use the foot of the Stimpson's surf clam in a sushi dish called *hokkigai*. This clam has a hard shell. It is also called the Arctic surf clam.

very much like the clam chowder we eat today. Clams can be eaten fried, steamed, or over pasta, too. Linguine with clam sauce is a favorite pasta dish from Italy. People also use clams as bait to catch other fish.

CLAMS AND OUR WORLD

Changes in the environment, no matter how small, can be a danger for even the healthiest species of clam. Today, one of the biggest dangers to clams is overharvesting by people.

As one of the longest-living animals on Earth, clams give us a picture of what our oceans were like hundreds of years ago. By studying their

If you visit a beach, look for clams. This kid found a giant clam's shell while swimming in the South Pacific Ocean!

shells, people can see how changes in the environment will shape life in our oceans hundreds of years from now.

GLOSSARY

bivalve (BY-valv) Having two shells.

byssus (BY-sus) The threadlike things with which some animals that live in water fix themselves to rocks.

coral reefs (KOR-ul REEFS) Underwater hills of coral.

gills (GILZ) Body parts that fish and other animals use for breathing.

larvae (LAHR-vee) Animals in an early period of life.

mantle (MAN-tel) A body part that covers other parts.

mollusks (MAH-lusks) Animals without backbones and with soft bodies and, often, shells.

mudflats (MUD-flats) Flat, muddy places that the sea covers part of the time.

overharvested (oh-ver-HAHR-vest-ed) Picked, caught, or gathered too many times.

oxygen (OK-sih-jen) A gas that has no color or taste and is necessary for people and animals to breathe.

plankton (PLANK-ten) Plants and animals that drift with water currents.

siphons (SY-funz) Tube-shaped body parts used for taking in or spraying out water.

species (SPEE-sheez) One kind of living thing. All people are one species.

INDEX

WEB SITES

Due to the changing nature of Internet links, PowerKids Press has developed an online list of Web sites related to the subject of this book. This site is updated regularly. Please use this link to access the list:
www.powerkidslinks.com/alsh/clams/